For those who painted these signs so many years ago, your signs remind us of our quickly disappearing architectural and industrial past.

Thank you to Claude.

Ghost Signs
of
Madison, Wisconsin

Second Edition

by
Maureen Janson Heintz

Table of Contents

All photos and text by Maureen Janson Heintz.

Introduction

Many faded advertising signs that still haunt the sides of old buildings, predate billboards and signs of today. Often referred to as ghost signs, most of these were hand-painted directly on building exteriors, a common practice between the late 1800s and the 1930s. From fancy graphics and images to simple announcements of a company name, some have been restored and repainted to look like the original. Many have been left to deteriorate with time and weather. Truly ghostly are those on which the paint has completely disappeared from the building surface leaving only cleaner brick where the images or words once were.

By the time this reaches your hands, there is no guarantee that any of the signs in this book are still visible, or that they will be in the near future. Sadly, some ghost signs have been defaced by vandals. Many are covered all or in part by foliage and most will continue to fade. Since my first edition of this book in 2013, a number of them have been concealed by new construction or demolished entirely.

In this volume, somewhat of a field guide to Madison ghost signs, each sign is named by its legible words. Grouped geographically, the signs are presented in an order traveling from the east side of Madison, through downtown, and continuing through the west side. Only signs painted directly onto the surface bricks or exterior of a building are featured here. The address of each sign location is provided, but the signs may be on the sides, and in some cases, the backs of the buildings. Assorted anecdotes of information about the origin of the signs, architecture, people or businesses that once occupied the buildings accompany the photos.

Madison Ghost Signs

Madison is home to nearly 40 ghost signs as of this printing in 2018. Some of them are easily spotted, while others take some effort to find or notice. The signs vary in legibility, some have been repainted with great clarity and some loom like true ghosts, nearly faded from sight. Included here are a few partial signs, as well as some very very faded signs, illegible in some cases, and at least one sign which can no longer be seen.

When I published the first edition of this book in 2013, within a year, I realized that the ghost sign landscape was rapidly changing. Seemingly every week, new signs were being revealed and old signs were being covered up or destroyed. Each time I thought about revising the book to reflect those changes, I realized I'd probably never be able to keep up. Even signs that are currently exposed are subject to the deterioration that weather brings. So each edition of this book will include signs that I documented since I first began this project in 2012 as well as newly revealed signs and updates on those that are no longer visible.

The majority of Madison signs are found east of the Capitol square, primarily along the old railroad corridor. There's a sprinkling of them around the Capitol and down State Street, representing advertisements. And a few more spill out on the near west side rail corridor labeling old and historic warehouses and industrial sites. It's likely that a few ghost signs still haunting Madison have not been included in this book, so keep an eye out for undiscovered signs. Along with finding these signs comes a chance to appreciate architecture and increase awareness of the history of the city of Madison.

East Side

Garvers Supply Co.
Entrance
Madison Brass Works, Inc.
Iron Works, Inc.
Madison Kipp Corporation
Community Laundry
Scanlan-Morris
The Ohio Chemical & Mfg. Co.
Real Estate Ross M. Koen Realty Co.
Straus Printers
Madison Dairy Produce
Eastside Cleaners, 7up
Bock Corporation
Madison Fireproof Warehouse
Gardner Baking Co.
Tavern
Furniture
Star Food Shop, Fresh Gardner's Purity
Krause Grocery Meats, King Midas Flour
Madison Candy Co.
International Harvester Company of America
Machinery Row

Garvers Supply Co.
3300 Sugar Ave.

Long abandoned, this building behind Olbrich Gardens is under major rennovation upon this printing. The faint ghost signs here still appear on two sides of the building, one side facing the railroad tracks and bike path, and the other on the graffiti-covered west side of the building. Until construction is complete, there is no way of knowing how much still be visible.

Originally built between 1902 and 1904 for the U. S. Sugar Company, this was a beet sugar refinery until 1924 when the company went bankrupt. According to different sources, it was either 1929 or 1931 when the building was purchased by James R. Garver, and operated as an agricultural supply company.

Entrance
2926 Atwood Ave.

The sign on the back of this old hotel building is barely readable. The words "entrance" and "park" are visible, as is an arrow pointing toward the back of the building. It's uncertain what this sign originally announced, but perhaps it was the parking lot of Weinschel's Department Store which occupied the building from 1930-1968. The sign has been painted on the back of what was originally built in 1904 as a hotel, first named Schlitz, and later Fair Oaks Hotel. It is currently home to an appliance store.

Madison Brass Works, Inc.
214 Waubesa St.

In 1907, a German named Henry Vogts and his relative Edward Schwenn started Madison Brass Works, making brass castings that were shipped out to manufacturing companies in Madison, Racine, Milwaukee, and Chicago. The building pictured here was constructed in 1917 after the original Brass Works wooden building burned to the ground. The current occupant, Goodman Community Center, has all but demolished the building. Yet they were careful to preserve this wall and magnificent sign.

Iron Works Inc.
149 Waubesa St.

Don't be fooled by the painted sign on the front of this long warehouse announcing the Goodman Community Center. That sign is new! But walk yourself around the length of the building to the back side, near the railroad tracks, and look beyond the back gate. There you'll find the original (retouched) signage for Iron Works, Inc. The left end of this sign is obstructed by building renovations, and this same signage used to appear on the front of the building, now painted over by the Goodman Community Center. Kupfer Ironworks operated in this building from 1940-1985 creating, among other things, steel beams for highway bridges.

This sign is actually on the back of the large Madison-Kipp building, and is best viewed by taking a short walk down the bike path just behind the Waubesa St. headquarters, and right across the street from Brass Works, Goodman Community Center. Look carefully to see the smaller words "die" and "casting" at the bottom of the sign.

Madison-Kipp Corporation has been making mechanical devices for lubricating large engines on Madison's east side since 1903, and expanded into the Atwood building (the former Four Lakes Ordnance Company built in 1917) in 1937. They also produce zinc and aluminum die casting machines and a pneumatic grinder.

Community Laundry
514 Division St.

Spreading wide across the facade of this building, this sign is often obscured by semi trucks parked in front of it. Little information exists on the history of this building and its signage. Above the larger words can be seen the smaller "family washing", and "dry cleaning". Community Laundry operated here from 1925-1935 before moving to a different location on the east side. It is currently used by Schoepp's Ice Cream plant which occupies several buildings in the neighborhood.

Scanlan-Morris
1902 E. Johnson St.

Thomas S. Morris and Samuel Gwyn Scanlan began a medical supply company in the early 1900s. Scanlan apparently invented the first hydraulically raised and lowered operating table built in the U.S. Their first facility was in the Machinery Row neighborhood, and as the business grew, they moved further east to this larger building at East Johnson St. and Pennsylvania Ave. The original building on this site was destroyed by fire in 1914 and immediately rebuilt.

This huge warehouse shows signs of the Scanlan-Morris occupancy on almost every exterior wall of the building, despite that Morris withdrew from the company in 1908. A few of the name signs are pictured here, and it's fun to saunter around and see if you can spot them all! The building is currently occupied by several tenants as warehouse and storage space.

15

The Ohio Chemical & Mfg. Co.
E. Johnson St. and Pennsylvania Ave.

When Scanlan of Scanlan-Morris retired in 1944, the company was absorbed by the larger Cleveland-based Ohio Chemical and Manufacturing Company. The sign on this building, right next to the Scanlon-Morris empire, still remains.

Real Estate Ross M. Koen Realty Co.
1257 E. Johnson St.

Sandwich yourself between the woodcrafters shop currently at this location, and the apartment building next door for a sign that is otherwise not easily seen. Painted in the shape of a house, the upper part of the sign is in tact, while the lower part has been vandalized and is more worn. This building was constructed in 1925, the same year that Ross Koen acted as the agent for the sale of the Fuller's Woods subdivision, now a part of Maple Bluff on Madison's east side. He operated his realty business until 1933.

Straus Printers and Lithographers
1002 E. Washington Ave

This sign for Straus Printers and Lithographers existed very very near to the neighboring building. Here, part of the sign was painted over, and the rest nearly impossible to see. The building and sign were completely demolished in 2016, but the company now called Suttle-Straus still operates from it's base in Waunakee.

Madison Dairy Produce
1002 E. Washington Ave

On the other side of the Straus Printers building, this sign saw the light of day for a few hours in 2016. When Madison Dairy Produce took over the building some time in the late 1930s or early 40s, they advertised here. Later they built an addition to this building covering up this wall completely with their new wing. During demolition, the new section of the building came down first, revealing this sign. A few hours later, these walls also came tumbling down.

Eastside Cleaners Tailoring Altering, 7up
836 E. Johnson St.

Formerly Rick's Cafe, and then Madison International Market, and now a used clothing store, there is little other documented about this sign's history. It's hard to know if this building was actually the site of a cleaning business, or just a place for this advertising sign. Dense with foliage, this sign appears at street-level, virtually on the front lawn of the house next door. Also, despite it's large and colorful appearance, you might miss this one if you were driving by. The sign initially would have greeted you on this road, had you been traveling west, but Johnson is a one-way street traveling east. It's best to find this one on foot. Not in the greatest condition, its easy access at the ground level has made this sign a target for graffiti.

Bock Corporation
110 S. Dickinson St.

Oscar Bock started a business making oil burners as an alternative to burning coal as a source of heat. Established in 1929, Bock Corporation still occupies this warehouse where they manufacture a wide range of water heaters.

Madison Fireproof Warehouse
825-827 E. Washington Ave.

According to Wisconsin Historical Society records, this nondescript red brick building initially built in 1912, packed and stored furniture and furs, and had special vault storage rooms for silver, valuable papers, and pianos. The business also cleaned carpets and sold second-hand furniture. No longer an empty lot next door, this sign is only partially visible from the street now, but can still be seen up close between it and the new building next door.

Newly revealed just prior to the emply lot development, on the front of this same building is the word Storage where there previously hung signage for A-1 Storage. Concealed under the newer hanging sign kept this one in reasonable condition.

Gardner Baking Co.
849 E. Washington Ave.

A savvy young baker named Louis Gardner came to Madison in 1928 and founded the Gardner Baking Company. In this building, he used machinery that could produce 50,000 loaves of his Purity white bread to supply the region. (Purity Bread is featured on the sign at 1053 Williamson St.) Now called Gardner's Bakery, the business moved further east on Washington Ave, where it remains today. Signs are on both the east and west side of this building.

Tavern
1524 Williamson St.

Originally the Yahara Hotel, built in 1902, this building houses the oldest tavern in Madison. It's not clear when the sign was painted, as it does not appear in photos of the original hotel. But its worn nature suggests it's been there for a while.

Furniture
1106 Williamson St.

When this private home underwent recent rennovation, with the removal of a coat of white paint, some signage was uncovered. Apparently there were more words below the bottom windows, but the owners decided to preserve and restore only the upper word.

Star Food Shop, Fresh Gardner's Purity
1053 Williamson St.

One of the most visible signs in Madison, advertising Gardner's Fresh Purity bread (of Gardner Baking Co.), this sign appears on the side of the former Berkan's Grocery Store. The store was owned and operated by Baraboo native, Jules Berkan, until his retirement in 1945. The name remained until 1952 when it was changed to Star Food Shop. This sign has been well preserved but somewhere in the refurbishing process the letter G in Gardner's was left incomplete and appears as a letter C.

Originally the Biederstadt-Breitnebach corner grocery store was built in 1874. It is not certain as to whether or not it became Krause Grocery & Meats, or if Krause advertised on the side of a competitors store.

King Midas Flour was branded in the early 1900's so the sign came no earlier than that. The Minnesota based Peavey Company bought King Midas in 1928, moving from the east coast base of Pennsylvania. This, perhaps, lead to increased advertising in the Midwest, so it's possible the sign was painted sometime in the late 1920's or early 1930's. The Biederstadt-Breitnebach grocery store, which is now in the National Register of Historic Places, operated until 1951.

31

Madison Candy Co.
744 Williamson St.

This sign appears on the two sides of the building, announcing the headquarters of the Madison Candy Company which was established in 1899. The company, started by Joseph E. Kleiner, produced popular candy, cheese, nuts, crackers and even cigars! They moved near to the railroad and into this factory building when it was built in 1903. In 1927, the company ceased operations, and in 1946, Ela Welding Supplies moved into the building, but the Madison Candy Co. sign remained. Repainted at some point, perhaps during a recent building renovation and listed in the National Register of Historic Places, it is now the home of, among other businesses, the Eldorado Grill, a popular Mexican restaurant.

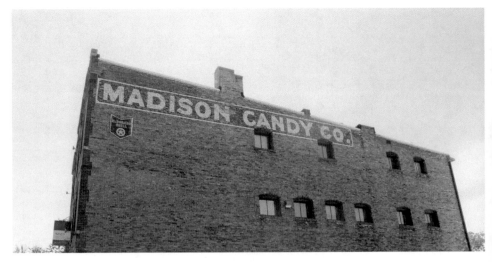

International Harvester Company of America
301 S. Blount St.

The front corner of this building (the south end of Blount St.) has vertical "oil tractors" sign. The back side has been remodeled adding an entrance from the parking lot, which covers some of the original sign, although what remains is quite impressive. Originally built in 1898, this facility housed branch offices of McCormick Harvest Machine Company and International Harvester. The companies sold and distributed farm machinery and implements. When they merged to become International Harvester Company in 1902, the building was expanded, and the signs were repainted. A portion of the photo at right (bottom) shows evidence of the word "McCormick" under newer lettering. The building remained International Harvester until 1953, and in 2010, gained a spot in the National Register of Historic Places.

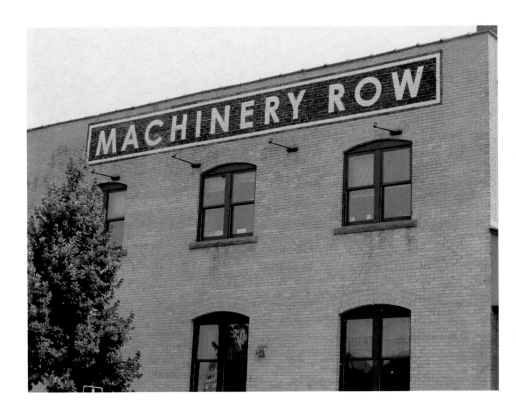

Because this building underwent a renovation, a lot of historical information has been gathered about it. This warehouse was originally the site of wooden tobacco and ice houses, whose booming businesses gave the area the title of Machinery Row. A portion of Machinery Row sustained a fire in 1912, and was rebuilt shortly thereafter. Built in sections between the years 1898 and 1902, the building now houses a bicycle store, a high-end restaurant, a yoga studio, and numerous other businesses. The sign has been repainted, announcing the name of the building, and is highly visible from eastbound John Nolen Drive.

Downtown

Findlay Groceries, Spear Head
New Belmont Hotel
Bank of Madison
Barons
YWCA Cafeteria
Universal
No Parking Fire Zone
Beer/Fauerbach CB
Illegible
Spiegel Catalog Shopping Center
Drink Coca Cola
Furnished Rooms for Rent

Findlay Groceries, Spear Head
203-207 King St.

Findlay Groceries, run by Alexander Findlay, was one of the largest groceries and food suppliers in Madison and provided for the city as well as other towns in Dane County. The building was constructed in 1882. The words "spear head" refer to Spear Head Tobacco, manufactured in the late 1800s, with its arrow-shaped logo shown beneath the words. The slightly enhanced photo below shows the top of the sign a bit more clearly.

New Belmont Hotel
101 E. Mifflin St.

A very faint sign remains on the New Belmont Hotel, built in the 1920s. The building is listed in the National Register or Historic Places. Its height prompted the creation of a legislation protecting the view of the capital by restricting the height of new construction. Operating as a hotel until 1968, it is now a YWCA. This sign is best viewed from a distance.

Bank of Madison
1 E. Main St.

The Bank of Madison building at 1 E. Main St was established in 1923. Just across from the Capitol, this building is about as central is it can get. But this particular sign missed the first edition of this book simply because it is difficult to see. From the first block on the east side of Martin Luther King, Jr. Blvd., look up until you see the central tower unit of this building. Surprise! Faded, and barely legible, there it is.

Barons
12 W. Mifflin St.

Another faint, and surprising sign on the Capitol square, this one can't be seen unless you are facing opposite the direction of car traffic. Here was the home of Baron's Department Store, owned and operated by two brothers. The popular store opened in this location in 1922. Best seen from across the street, the sign also reveals barely visible words "department store" and to the right, likely the words "eagle stamps". A few more details appear in the darker photo below.

YWCA Cafeteria
122 State St.

Before moving into the New Belmont Hotel, the YWCA was located at 122 State St. There are signs on two sides of this building announcing the cafeteria, which was apparently open to the public. The YWCA hosted classes for women including bowling, tennis and golf lessons. The 1917 architecture is no longer obvious, except for the signs, since a new facade was put on the building in 1971. Rumor has it this building will soon be gone, and the signs disappear as well.

Universal
115 State St.

Here's an example of a sign that revealed itself during recent demolition of the building next door. Unfortunately, it is no longer visible. Only on display for a short time, the photos here show a series of its disappearance. Many ghost signs have suffered the same fate, so there may be more among us that we will never see until the wall next door comes down. This sign, although partial, is an advertisement for Duluth Universal Flour, a company that operated out of northern Minnesota from about 1900-1958.

No Parking Fire Zone
State St.

This sign doesn't advertise anything, but I still consider this one a ghost sign, and a secret one at that! Located inside a building in the downtown area, it's in an enclosed hallway connecting the old portion of a building with a new portion that was completed in 2004. If you are lucky, you might just be able to come across this one someday.

These two awesome signs were recently revealed right at street level, after siding was removed from what was the former Fontana Sports store (now Short Stack Eatery). Although the building address is 301 W. Johnson, these signs are on the Henry St. side of the building.

The sign at the left most likely reads, Schlitz, the Beer that Made Milwaukee Famous. What you can see here is the only visible section, although it's possible that more of the sign might someday be revealed above. The sides have been replaced by windows.

The sign at right is for the local Fauerback Centennial Brew. This particular beer was introduced by the brewery in 1948.

Not much is visible or known about this sign, other than its place on the west side of the 427 State St. building. Since this building once housed a Spiegel Catalog office (see p. 49), it's possible that is says something related to that.

Eva Lauffer Deutschkron and Martin Deutschkron once owned a business called Martin's, a mens tailoring shop, in this location, but that was in the 1950s, and it's likely that this sign has been there since well before Martin's.

Spiegel Catalog Shopping Center
328 W. Gorham St.

Covered by a hanging billboard for a number of years, this intriguing sign was recently revealed. The lights remain from the previous billboard. In the 1930s and 40s, Speigel had a catalog order office at 427 State St. which is actually the same building as this address on Gorham St.

Drink Coca Cola
501 State St.

Peek around the back side of the Tudor revival 1901 building (currently Stop & Shop) and you'll find a ghost sign on top of a ghost sign. Drink Coca Cola is legible here, layered over what looks like an earlier Coca Cola advertisement.

Eye-level and small, this sign could be easily missed. Definitely best found on foot, it sits on the west side of the building, which is still an apartment building. The year of this sign is unknown.

West Side

Sunkist
Wiedenbeck Dobelin Co.
P. Lorillard Company
Gallagher Tent Co.
Dr. Wahl. Physician & Surgeon
Royal Crown
Fix
Coca-Cola Delicious and Refreshing
Illegible
Meier's Garage

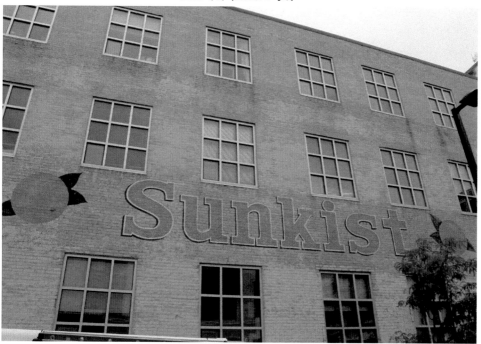

On a west side rail-corridor warehouse, this 1929 sign has been restored recently. Before restoration, the sign was so faded, it was only visible after a rainfall. The Whole Produce Company run by the Heilman family, was housed here for a time, until going belly-up in the depression of the 1930s.

Wiedenbeck Dobelin Co.
615 W. Mifflin St.

Freshly painted and restored, this sign is easy to spot from West Washington Ave. A hardware business was housed here in the early 1900s, along with a wholesale blacksmith and a wagon-making operation. Built between 1907 and 1915, it is one of the last surviving warehouse buildings along this near west rail corridor. Of architectural note, the building owns historic designation, and now holds upscale student apartments.

P. Lorillard Company
651 W. Doty St.

The P. Lorillard building complex is very large, and has three different signs visible on it. Although the building interiors have been converted into apartments, the signs have not been restored. Some will be more obvious than others. Originally built as the American Tobacco Company warehouses in 1899, the buildings were later occupied by the P. Lorillard Tobacco Company, producers of Kent, Old Gold, and True brand cigarettes. Surrounded by tobacco farms, Madison was a prime location for tobacco warehouses, particularly those constructed near the Milwaukee Road and Illinois Central rail yards in this neighborhood. Tobacco production declined between 1930 and 1950, requiring fewer warehouses.

John Gallagher Co.
305 S. Bedford St.

305 S. Bedford

There are two signs here. Both require careful scrutiny to discover. A portion of this building was constructed in 1914 as the Gallagher Tent and Awning Factory. Another part was built in 1921 as the Frank Brothers Fruit Company, an expansion produce distribution facility of the Frank Brothers Grocery, now the Frank Beverage Group. One faded sign is a true ghost sign, haunting the building only from certain angles. The other sign on the parking lot side has was restored at some point (as seen below photographed in 2013), and then subsequently painted over (see next page), advertising the Gallagher Company which still exists in a different location.

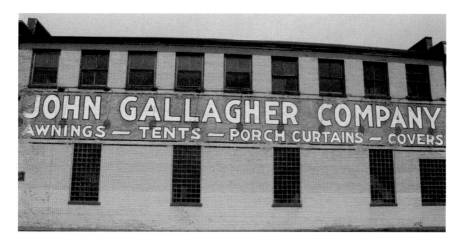

JOHN GALLAGHER COMPANY
AWNINGS — TENTS — PORCH CURTAINS — COVERS

In 2014, new building owners decided to paint over the iconic sign. But if you look carefully, you will still see a hint of the lettering beneath the yellow paint.

Another small eye-level sign, this one is best spotted on foot. You may never see it by car, as it faces opposite the one-way traffic direction here. One of the most unique signs in Madison, the history of this and of Dr. Wahl is undocumented.

A little bit of detective work points to this sign as most likely a Royal Crown Cola advertisement. Other such advertisements for RC Cola with similar design exist, most of which are smaller and made of tin. It's possible to vaguely see the word "drink" on the upper left corner of this sign. The photo below was slightly darkened to show the larger words more clearly.

Sometimes you have to shimmy and squeeze yourself between buildings in order to see a ghost sign. With this one, it's impossible, as the new building next door left no space to do so. From the sidewalk the word "fix" appears (last photo), and a few other partial words are clear, but the full text is not decipherable.

Coca-Cola Delicious and Refreshing
109 E. Lakeside St.

This Coca-Cola sign has been exposed to the elements for a long time, but the trademark logo and words "delicious and refreshing" are still visible upon careful scrutiny. This spot was once home to the Lakeside Grocery famous for selling Kennedy's Velvet Ice Cream.

Some may not even think this is a sign, but there are very faint outlines of letters present here. Illegible and visible only from very specific angles, this sign is buried off the beaten path and nearly behind the adjoining yellow building, a section of the current Budget Bicycle Center. This building is the former Klein Dickert Paint store where windows were also sold. Looking closely the name Dickert can be partially seen.

Meier's Garage
1313 Regent St.

Still home to an auto garage, this ivy-covered sign announces the original business in the building. Meier's Garage opened here in 1920 and later moved and expanded, operating now as Meier Truck Fleet Repair. A renovation in 2016 brought a lovely surprise: another sign on the east side of the building!

Tips on Ghost Sign Hunting

-The best and safest ways to hunt ghost signs are on foot or by bike. Some signs can be found on bike paths that are built along former railroad tracks.

-Look up, look down, some are on street or eye level, some are at the tops of buildings.

-Sometimes it's easier to spot faint signs from farther away or on an overcast day.

-Look between buildings.

-Look on the back or sides of buildings. And look on the far side of buildings that are on one-way streets. In some cases, your nearest sign may be behind you.

-Wear polarized sunglasses. The glasses may enable you to see a faint ghost sign better, particularly those that remain on cleaner bricks where there once was paint.

-Look in the winter or spring--before ivy and other plants and trees are in bloom, sometimes obscuring signs.

-Look near and far. You can often see far away signs that were obstructed by other buildings when you were close.

-Go with a friend. Two pairs of eyes are usually better than one!

-Check out construction sites. Sometimes building demolition can reveal on old sign. Also keep in mind that with new development, sometimes a sign you see now maybe covered by new construction in the near future.

References

Bock Water Heaters, Company History, http://www.bockwaterheaters.com/CompanyInformation/History

Historic Madison, Inc. Walking Tours, Walking and Biking Tours in Several Industrial Areas of Madison, Wisconsin, 1880-1970 , http://www.historicmadison.org/Madison's%20Past/Industrial%20Areas/Industrial%20Tours.pdf

Wikipedia, McCormick-International Harvester Company Branch House, http://en.wikipedia.org/wiki/McCormick-International_Harvester_Company_Branch_House, "Weekly List of Actions Taken On Properties". National Park Service. Retrieved 2012-02-06. "McCormick-International Harvester Company Branch House". Wisconsin Historical Society. Retrieved 2012-02-06.

Frank Beverage Group, http://www.frankbeveragegroup.com/history/

Machinery Row, owned and operated by Seven Js. http://www.machinery-row.com/history.php

City of Madison Landmarks Commission, Landmarks and Landmark Sites Nomination Form (1), http://www.cityofmadison.com/planning/landmark/nominations/117_3244AtwoodAve.pdf

Dave Zweifel, " Dave Zweifel's Madison: Community Shares Unveils Nonprofit Collaboration at its New Center for Change, The Cap Times, August 30, 2011.

Wisconsin Historical Society, preview site, http://preview.wisconsinhistory.org/Content.aspx?dsNav=Nrc:id-4294966613,N:4294966686-4294966508-4294963781&dsNavOnly=N:4294953747

Historic Madison, Inc., the Origins of Some Madison, Wisconsin Street Names, http://www.historic-madison.org/Madison's%20Past/Street%20Names/PartXI.html

City of Madison, Shenk's-Atwood: A Walking Tour, brochure, http://www.cityofmadison.com/planning/landmark/SchenkAtwoodWalkingTour.pdf

Maximum Ink, Music Magazine, http://www.maximumink.com/index.php/calendar/permalink/mickeys_tavern

Chris Martell, Historic Mickey's Tavern Starts Serving Food , 77 Square, November 11, 2007

Jay Rath, The Ghost Signs of Madison, Isthmus, August 15, 2013

About Ghost Signs, Dr. Ken Jones, http://www.drkenjones.com/ghostsigns/AboutGS.php

Wisconsin Historical Society, Wisconsin Local History & Biography Articles, http://www.wisconsinhistory.org/wlhba/articleView.asp?pg=4&orderby=&id=15224&pn=1&adv=yes&hdl=&np=&ln=Morris&fn=T%2E&q=&y1=&y2=&ci=&co=&mhd=&shd=

City of Madison, Historic Resources of Downtown Madison, http://www.cityofmadison.com/planning/histresc.pdf

Earl Reichel, Madison Resident

Meier Truck and Fleet Repair, http://meiertruckservice.com

Here's a mystery sign on the side of the 1216 Williamson St. building (originally Karl's Meat Market). This photo has been darkened, but still not readable...Do you know what it says?

Spot a ghost sign in Madison that's not shown in this book? Do you know what any of the illegible signs actually say? Let us know by way of email, and we'll include it in the next edition!

ghostsignsofmadison@gmail.com

About the Author

Maureen Janson Heintz is an artist and writer living in Madison, Wisconsin. She enjoys ghost sign hunting wherever she goes.

Made in the USA
Monee, IL
31 October 2020